Shadow Glimpses

by

Charlotte Ann Caprio

authorHOUSE

1663 LIBERTY DRIVE, SUITE 200
BLOOMINGTON, INDIANA 47403
(800) 839-8640
www.authorhouse.com

First published by AuthorHouse 04/08/04

ISBN: 1-4184-0851-4 (e)
ISBN: 1-4184-0853-0 (sc)
ISBN: 1-4184-0852-2 (dj)

Printed in the United States of America
Bloomington, Indiana

This book is printed on acid-free paper.

OUTSTANDING PRAISE FOR
SHADOW GLIMPSES

"This wonderful collection of poems reminds us of the really important things in life.....Our one true love, as well as those simple things that give meaning to our lives."

-------Hazel Catinella

"High praise for Charlotte's debut collection of poetry.....A shared wealth of feelings."

------J Henry

"Charlotte is a poet with heart and soul. A must for all women and men to read. I loved watching her story unfold in rhyme. A great talent."

-------Dolores Allen Author

"The poetry is for all women who have suffered. She gives hope for a brighter tomorrow. Thank you Charlotte...."

-------Denise Parks

"Charlotte's poems inspire me, allowing me to feel good about myself after reading them and assist me in thinking about the many blessings I have."

--------Diane Edstrand

"To my husband Jim, whose faith and love made this book possible"

And

"And for my grandchildren, who gave me a reason to push forward"

And

"Last but not least to all my wonderful friends, who stood by me and said "Go for it.""

Table of Contents

Changes In Time

Everything changes in its time:
The heart and soul,
And even one's mind.

Nothing can stay as once it was,
Even the heavens change,
Within the clouds above.

We grow older as time rushes by,
Nothing can change this,
We can only try.

Yet we grow wiser in what we have learned,
Cannot forget the past,
Or the goals we once yearned.

We searched for ourselves,
Looking deeply within,
Finding truths above all else in the end;

Cannot foresee what is yet to be had,
But know above all else,
Must take the good with the bad.

For time changes all,
The past and the present,
Filling our souls within with its essence.

The heart and soul,
And even one's mind,
Cannot escape the truth of time.

When I Grow Old

Dedicated to: The love of my life, James Caprio

When I grow old,
And am no longer attractive,
Will you still love me,
Even when my mind is lacking?

When I grow old,
And my hair is all gray,
Will you still love me,
As on that first day?

When I grow old,
And my skins's all wrinkled,
Will you still love me,
Crooks, crannies and crinkles?

When I grow old,
And am no longer a young chick,
Will you still love me,
As you write the Medicare check?

When I grow old,
And the passion's not there,
Just remember my love,
I was the one always there.

Land Of Myth

As the softest of breezes rushes through the leaves,
Life moves forward in this land of myth with ease.
The sun shines its rays of light upon the rivers,
As the waters rush over the pebbled bottom forever.

A kind of hush seems to lie across this land,
From where one might find at last a way to descend.
There are fairies with the most colorful of wings,
And if you but listen, will hear their tiny voices sing.

They sing of the spirit which lies in everyone,
Laughing and enjoying the beauty of the sun.
For here the greenest greens and bluest blues are had,
Leaving ones heart filled with such joy never to feel sad.

Animals of every kind and shape live together in peace,
Mysteries to be found in such wonder if one but believes.
Never again to be silenced as once centuries ago was,
But now to find those quiet wonders and now only trust.

For within the breeze however one might feel or see,
Life moves forward if we look within and truly believe.
Look to the spirits of joy and lauher that flow with ease,
Give it your all and listen, for there's much to receive.

This Is My Time

To feel the wind against one's face,
To share the joys of love and grace,
To be as one with an inner peace,
This is my time, this is my place.

To sail with the wind high above,
To taste salt from tears of love,
To escape turmoil deep within the core,
This is my song, this is what life is made of.

To be unmeasured by another's heart,
To find sanctuary and never depart,
To feel joy within from the song of a lark,
This is my time, this is my start.

To accept the one you have become,
To never feel loneliness nor ever alone,
To sense what's inside right or wrong,
And to come closer, feeling the warmth of the sun.

This is my time, this is my place,
This is my world, sailing with grace.
This is my love, this is my heart,
A life filled with love, a wondrous new start.

Mystical Dust

Mystical dust from a cloud,
Enter within its realm.
Coming closer all about,
Find the magic to descend.

Discover that which gives light,
Life just beyond our grasp.
Within seems so bright,
Dare to see it, dare to ask.

Worthy of touching or feeling,
Sanctuary where there is none.
Hiding yet all concealing,
Knowing the cloud is where it begun.

Sensing something more than forever,
Gently caressing the heart in its wake.
Becoming wary, sharp as a dagger,
Must accept, lest feel the ache.

Mystical dust seems to bring life,
Life no longer beyond one's grasp.
Nothing ever felt quite so precise,
Now have found it, I need not ask.

The Sea

Carry me out to sea;
That's the magical place to be,
Where mermaids and birds do play.
There we will find a bright day.

Explore the treasures below,
Where no winds harshly blow.
Escape the turmoil of life unknown,
For here I will find a mystical song.

Singing and making merry,
Never sensing cold nor wary.
For there's time for joy and fun,
All on the beams of the sun.

The waves crash merrily all around,
Yet unheard, without a sound.
For peace and tranquility lie close by,
Wrapping you in its warmth deep inside.

A dance of light and shadow join to play,
Here you will find a beautiful day.
For the mermaids and birds sing and have fun,
Now have found a magical place in the sun.

Essence of Being

To sense the essence of life,
Feeling it deep to the core;
For within the life force stirs,
Awareness becoming much more.

Allowing acceptance of what is to be,
Yet bringing you closer that you might see.
Facing that this is truth even if unsure,
No more locks, no more doors.

Freedom is within your grasp,
Need never beg nor to ask.
For within the force of life there is light,
Filling you with a sense so bright,

Capturing your heart and soul,
Giving you life, making you whole.
No more tears left unshed,
For within life nothing is left unsaid.

Sleep Tight

Wish I may and wish I might,
I've said this wish on many a dark night.
As I was tucked in and said my prayers,
I waited for the fates to at last interfere.

Yet never before have I felt their wisdom,
For at last have found what I was missing;
Can still follow what was known to be true,
Yet there is still so much more to pursue.

Wishes and prayers there were so many,
But in my heart wondered if there were any.
Would what I wanted and needed come to be,
And would I finally begin to see?

All that once was has at last disappeared,
And my heart feels light and will no longer despair,
Have gone beyond and found love at last,
This could never have happened in the past.

For what I have now comes only with age,
Finding myself able to write of love page after page.
When at last love is found and held so deep,
Your heart awakens, never again to sleep.

Winds

As the night wind blows,
And all seems quiet,
Listen carefully,
To the heart taking flight.

For here will know,
Just what you seek,
The world as it is,
Be it yours to keep.

Time to explore,
For now is the time,
Even if life seems,
At times unkind.

Follow your dreams,
And let your wings spread,
For the skies are clear,
No more a sense of dread.

The heart is opened,
And at last it hears,
All that is right;
It no longer fears.

Higher and higher,
You will reach above,
Here is your chance,
To hold and feel love.

A Storm Of Love

I see a storm brewing over the horizon,
The winds picking up, energy rising.
The limbs on the tree seem to sway in anger;
I hear a crackling, feel the danger.

No escape from this storm as it blows,
Sensing the harshness of the limbs as they bow.
Where is the sunshine once surrounding,
Where is the music, why is the heart pounding?

Within, the heart can feel such dread;
Why is the soul sinking as if it were dead?
Surviving the turmoil seems futile at times,
Yet there is an energy held deep inside.

I'll find that place before the storm,
Never allowing it to cause such harm.
For where there is love there is a chance,
I will find the light, will again sense.

Beyond the storm lies the rainbow,
Where winds caress, not blow.
Where birds sing and the heart is at peace,
A world of wonder is held in this place.

Love will again light the way to this beyond,
Where it will begin again as it once had begun.
Nothing can break the limbs if they give,
This is sanctuary, this is Love within.

Fire Of Life

As the fire burns in the grate,
A new life begins, for it's never too late.
Within the flames they burn with such haste,
Not much time left, nor any to waste.

Becoming aware to the core of your being,
Accepting the light that now you are seeing.
Turning each log as it becomes consumed,
Not wanting it to burn out, at least not too soon.

Warmth and contentment lay within that fire,
May last forever but unsure of the hour.
A quiet moment to just sit and ponder,
For within those flames lie a quiet wonder.

Where one log may burn into ash and cinders,
Can put another log on feeling a warmth so tender.
Quietly it burns on with much of life consumed,
Still wondering if maybe it's been much too soon.

But life lives on within those flames,
As smoke goes up the chimney with nothing to gain.
For outside the outer reaches of the hearth,
Nothing in life can be taken for granted nor rehearsed.

For the inner heart remains if one but allows,
As if smoke rising moving toward the clouds.
The heart of the flames becomes more apparent,
And life moves forward with the winds to steer it.

When Tomorrow Comes

When tomorrow comes and we aren't alone,
In each others arms we will be, whispering sweet nothings,
Knowing in our hearts this is where we belong,
The way it should be, aware and adjusting.

Swept away by our thoughts and dreams,
Being filled with love and laughter complete within,
Where the sun shines the brightest of beams,
This will go on forever after, knowing it's not the end.

For today and tomorrow will find new beginnings for us,
Giving of one another complete with no regrets,
Searching our hearts and souls with such trust,
Knowing what we feel is true and must not ever forget.

Not ever traveling the long lonely roads alone,
For within any storm a rainbow will guide us,
Together will find our place within that storm,
And in our hearts will follow and continue to trust.

So when tomorrow comes and we aren't alone,
Our hearts will sing the most wondrous of all songs,
At last finding our golden path in which to travel,
With all the mysteries that love will unravel.

A Mist

A fine mist comes over the land,
Leaving one intoxicated as it ascends.
To see the glistening of light upon the leaves,
A beauty once could not have seen.

For now have opened up to a whole new life,
Even if nothing's ever perfect nor precise.
And enlightenment of all that once was held within,
No longer fearing there being an end.

Light and shadow play such a part,
Filling the heart with a love to start.
Seeing all that lies just before you,
Experiencing the wonders of life so new.

Cannot remember now a time gone by,
When one could feel and sense so deeply inside.
Yet here it is at last in all its glory before you,
Reaching out and allowing love to be pursued.

A mist so fine that it just covers and gleams,
Bringing excitement within for you're no longer the same.
Love is like that new found beauty within the mist,
Where the heart will but glisten when you receive that first kiss.

Never again to be left alone in the dark,
For now the mist has taken over the heart.
Love is the light and the brightest to be found,
For one's heart now can hear such a wondrous sound.

Love Poem

With each beat of the heart,
And with each breath I take,
I will be by your side,
From mountain to lakes.

My love will only grow,
From here to forever,
From the highest clouds,
To the deepest seas.

Life with you gives light,
To the brightest star,
To the sun aglow,
So high and bright.

Never to feel loneliness,
From now to forever,
For within my heart,
You will live on forever.

There is but one love,
And now it is ours,
We have reached the stars,
Hearts filled with fire.

Sea Of Life

As the breeze flows,
Across the seas,
I've found that life,
Burns within me.

A time of joy,
Has yet to come,
To feel it flow,
Showing I belong.

For nowhere else,
Could there ever be,
Such wonders,
As found in me.

To spread my wings,
And sail on the wind,
In this I've found,
Life truly has begun.

Never to be left,
So far behind,
Now I've crossed,
Seas so sublime.

Capturing truths,
As yet untold,
For now in myself,
I've found my soul.

Sailing free,
To feel and be,
For now within,
Can clearly see.

A woman,
As yet unknown,
Now is the time to look,
And feel no longer alone.

Love and home,
Is held in the heart,
For this is truth,
Where it all must start.

Blank Pages

Where once I could write with hardly a try,
Now I stare at the screen just wondering why?
Why is it I feel blocked by all that surrounds,
Where are my feelings, where are the sounds?

I sense such a loss when I sit here waiting,
For nothing will come at all to these blank pages.
The love and light is just out of reach,
Yet there's so much more that I must seek.

Am I to open up so much more of myself,
Or is it better to leave it be or give more of self?
I can't understand why this has taken place,
All I see before me is empty space.

This is my way to start and end each day,
For this is for me still leaving me dismayed.
But here I am staring once again at a blank page,
I know it will come if I allow myself to find the way.

Day Of Horror

Dedicated to those who died on Sept. 11.

Sitting quietly and continuing to contemplate,
How did God allow such a horrific mistake?
Many lives we have seen destroyed this day,
And no one seems to have the right words to say.

Such horror has now come upon us,
Yet in this country we completely give our trust.
America stands for honor and freedom,
While terrorists come into our lives and condemn us.

Why should so many innocent lives be lost,
Are such terrors worth such a high cost?
No one should have to face such terror ever,
Once a life is taken it's completely forever.

Memories of what we have this day seen
Will be here for ages and will continue to be.
But America and its people will rise above,
For our country we will fight and remember,
What we are made of.

If I Were A Fairy

If I were a fairy,
From a far away land,
Could you still love me,
Hold me gently in your hand?
Caress me as once you did,
Whisper softly in my ear,
Sharing all those memories,
That we both hold so dear?
If I were a fairy,
From a far away land,
Would you still love me,
Do you really think you can?

And if I were to fly away,
How would you feel,
What would you say?
See beyond my fairy wings,
See inside my tiny heart,
So as time goes by,
And you really see me fly,
Don't be afraid, my love;
It will never hurt.
Just never ask why.
Let our lives intertwine,
And my wings will be yours,
Forevermore and so divine.
And you will always love me,
I know you really can.

Gift

I give to you my heart,
And I give to you my soul,
Wanting only to share,
And to let you know:

Nowhere else,
Would I rather be,
Then here beside you,
Just you and me.

Surrounded by love,
And knowing it's true,
This more then anything,
Is what I sense within you.

When the sun rises,
And shines on your face,
I know I have found,
Our special place.

Never again to feel alone,
Nor empty inside,
For I now know,
I belong by your side.

Together forever,
As lovers should be,
And within this light,
We'll always see.

The Final Caress

When rain falls from the heavens,
And tears caress my shoulders,
Giving me the sense of what is missed,
A love found within another.

The tears flow beyond control,
Unsure as to which is the path,
The journey seems so far from over,
Waiting to end, not meant to last.

Laughter till one can but cry,
This is worth giving all you can,
One must truly open the heart and try,
If the path is to be found again.

Like angelic music played upon a harp,
Can sense something special all around,
For within to the core of the heart,
Can feel the rhythm and hear the sound.

To come in from the rain,
Finding oneself and the place to begin,
Once done, nothing's ever the same,
Yet willing oneself to move once again.

Rain falling from the heavens,
Shows the way to begin,
For within that final caress,
Can find the path and the end.

Tomorrow

As you look out the window,
Wishing upon that first star,
You feel that the time will come,
There will be a brighter tomorrow.

For you sense the light within,
Never before wishing quite so hard,
Yet knowing this to be the time,
Ready to shed all sorrow.

Brightly shining the moon is aglow,
And you feel your soul as it soars,
To follow the path once unknown,
It can't wait for another tomorrow.

The brightness overcomes your heart,
Looking forward and never looking back,
Accepting the truths you once ignored,
Becoming enlightened, forgetting the sorrow.

The window is your outlook on truth,
So follow your heart as it must,
For the time has come to move forward,
For in tomorrows we can trust.

When You're Tired

When you become tired,
And worn to no end,
Think of the wonders in life,
Then you can ascend.

For within your reach,
There are colors in the rainbow,
To be had and held,
And enough life to fill your soul.

There to take you by the hand,
And lead you the right way,
For in this wondrous world,
There is much in a new day.

Caring and loving are here,
Filling the heart and soul,
Now you must move forward,
Finding a whole new goal.

Where the sun shines,
Lighting and dissolving the shadows,
Seeking that which is,
And knowing no more battles.

Forgetting to be tired,
And worn to no end,
For now the world is at last alive,
Spread your wings and ascend.

I Am Me

Should there be turmoil when you are right,
Is it so wrong to want love and to fight?
For never before have I been allowed,
To come from hiding behind a dark cloud.

At last I can sense exactly who I am,
Even if once didn't count within.
I am me with feelings and a wondrous soul,
Have journeyed far, for I knew I had to go.

Can others not see what it was that I went through,
At the time I didn't understand just what I was to do.
Never again will I be enslaved nor bond within,
For if I were, my heart and soul would die and end.

Escape came with a price of this I am sure,
Yet I yearned to be me and to feel secure.
Safe from where it was that I came,
Having found new love and nothing's to be the same.

For here I am rising high with the wind carrying me,
Feeling such love all around the way it should be.
Maybe for others what I did was wrong,
But in my heart can sing such wondrously new songs.

I am me and I deserve to be loved,
In my heart I know God sent it from above.
My time has come and I'll not leave,
Within my heart and soul will always believe.

I Wish For You

I wish for you as I wished then,
For love to spread its wings high on the wind,
Feeling and sensing the music within,
Finding my soul in flight, dancing again.

To find that which was always there,
Giving one the chance to become more aware.
Never to lose sight of the ground below,
As you dance upon the clouds all aglow.

I wish for you as I wished for you then,
Only warmth and love to be held in the heart,
Together as one dancing within the wind,
Hand in hand finding a new start.

For you are there and I am here,
A sense of the purest love held within,
Escape found in the music you hear,
Finding excitement in life without end.

Hearing the music deep to the core,
Two hearts together at last soar,
High upon the clouds above,
Now have found your wish filled with love.

A Magical Place

As I dance merrily alone,
My hair whipping in the breeze,
I've found within my heart and soul,
A sense of soaring free.

Excitement completely fills me,
Reaching deep to the core of my soul,
A light shines upon the path,
My heart is ready to go.

A wondrous place is awaiting,
Knowing it's my time to return,
My heart is shining brightly,
Have found that which I yearn.

The trees bow their branches,
Gesturing a welcome to me,
For this is a magical place,
Only a chosen few have ever seen.

The flowers in their wondrous clothes,
Colors glowing and waving their petals,
In this place one can only dream,
And knowing I'll not ever settle.

No longer a sense of uneasiness,
Nor any sorrow or tears.
For only love can dwell,
By leaving behind all fears.

The heart and soul can be,
Feeling such a sense of peace,
Dancing to your heart's delight,
Sensing so very much at ease.

Listening as the heart beats,
It's own rhythm quietly within,
For now I've found in my soul,
This wondrous magical land.

A place unlike any other,
Where one can completely just be,
Here within this magical world,
Now have peace and can soar free.

Changes

As a changeling can change its shape,
So can the heart once it has begun.
Opening up to another's love;
With forces moving you higher above.

To find the one you love and be allowed to give,
Knowing with this person you want to always live.
Making all your dreams and his come true,
This is what love has to offer to you.

New beginnings and a whole new way of being,
This more than anything is worthy of believing.
Once unable to express what is deeply felt within,
Now finding at last yourself and knowing you can.

To soar high above with your heart full of passions,
No longer afraid, it's all there for the asking.
Changes are many once love has been found,
Yet nothing ever again can feel quite so profound.

Yelling

Yelling out, "Hey world where are you?",
Show me your beauty, show me what's new.
Can you not share just a little with me?,
All I want is to see and believe.

Let me see what others seek,
Show me now that I might learn just to be.
I cannot understand all that's around,
And at times want to hear only the musical sounds.

Wishing I knew what life truly is all about,
Yet even within have many doubts.
Hey! let me in and show me what will soon be,
Can't move forward unless I can see.

I know there's not always good to be seen,
But my senses have yet to even conceive.
For out there I know there's so very much of life,
Even if it's not always within your world nice.

I want what others seem to have and hold dear,
And in my heart I feel that this is never quite fair.
To climb to the top and find all that is true,
This makes it a worthy journey in which to pursue.

To be allowed at last to sense and just be,
For in my world I am blind and want only to see.
Never to know what it is that has been missed,
Yet will accept all there is like the gentleness of a kiss.

For now I'm aware that there's so much more,
With just a turn of a knob can open the door.
Love is a beginning of this I am sure,
Believing in this world and at last feeling secure.

One's Place

A reminder of your place,
Comes when you least expect.
Just when you begin flying through space,
You find your wings have been clipped.

Brought back to earth,
When you only wanted to fly,
You can't understand,
Or fathom just why.

Tears of joy that once flowed,
No longer exist as the memories come.
Darkness comes over the soul,
Why can't it leave you alone?

Wanting only to love and be loved
For that which you are,
You feel the breeze in the air above,
A beautiful place by far.

Yet just when you sense you are,
A fallen angel you become;
For no matter just how far,
You are to quietly sit alone.

Never to completely understand,
But for now you continue to try.
One day we'll fly hand in hand,
In hopes the heart will be our guide.

To just love and be loved,
Is all one can truly ever want.
And within this time and space,
We'll soar and no longer feel alone.

Silence

A glimmer, a light,
Once shone in your eyes,
Now seems to be gone,
Guarded by dark skies.

The heart senses silence,
And no longer can hear,
Now deep within the core,
Feel a margin of fear.

Where once there was magic,
Now seems to have dissolved,
Not sure just when or how,
Was I the cause?

Once so open to all that is about,
Now my heart hurts,
Wanting to understand,
With no more doubts.

I know that you love me,
Of this I am sure,
And yet where is the light,
That kept me secure.

My love is completely yours,
From now till eternity,
All I ask is that you share,
And allow me to see.

I want more then anything,
To stay closely within your heart,
I knew it was love then,
And it still is as in the start.

I know not how to explain,
These feelings I have inside,
All I know in truth,
Is that I want you by my side.

To Know

Can one know the other
Completely heart and soul?
Can you sense the person,
Within, There is much to know.

What is it that draws one,
To seek out the other?
Is it the way one might reach out,
Or is it love felt for another?

The look that you see in another's eyes,
Brightly shining yet just a shadow.
The sense of the other's being,
Bringing you forward and allowing.

A space that was kept,
Now is closing as you watch,
Yet still in doubt,
But knowing within unable to stop.

Wanting only to be held,
Seeking out the one you want,
Never forgetting that you're more aware,
With nothing left to haunt.

For love is there in the shadow,
Shining brightly drawing you in,
Now that you have reached out,
Found a place in your heart to begin.

The Ship

When at last your ship sails,
Listen closely as the wind wails.
Awakening the senses to all about,
Raise up your voice and give a shout.

Beware of that which is held inside,
Keeping love close by your side.
Watch the clouds as they sail,
Held within the wind's gale.

Waters rise as if reaching out,
Waves reach high, fighting all about;
Turmoil and raging wars within reach,
Yet want only calm within to keep.

Nowhere to run nor a place to hide;
This is what is sensed deep inside,
Not knowing if light will ever come,
Yet sensing that soon I will see the sun.

Waters calm and silence fills the air,
Sun shines brightly with never a care.
A newness all about warm and filled with love,
A richness of life fills the skies above.

Gentle breezes begin to blow,
Birds fly high, knowing where they go;
Heart and soul at peace within,
The turmoil subsides, now at peace again.

The Sleep Of Unrest

A lullaby helps one sleep
Until the hour the dreamscape wakes;
With this dreary time of rest,
You breath the air of all the unjust.

Before that hour is over within,
You wish for it at last to end,
Never again to take over your dreams,
For not all in reality is as it seems.

Escape seems to come too slowly now,
Finding your way wondering just how
And who that other might come to be;
Within this dreamscape you must finally see.

An hour is much too long, you sense,
But you haven't time to move by chance;
Must find the portal that leads to the end,
Or else you will be lost and descend.

The time is nearly over now;
You're looking around, yet hearing no sound,
Awakening at last from that sleep of unrest,
Reality seeping in beyond the unmet.

Love Shared

I close my eyes,
Envisioning your face,
Knowing this time,
Knowing this place.

You gave me your heart,
Gave me your soul,
Held out your hand,
Made me whole.

Shared your love,
Gave me it all,
And in the end,
Knocked down my wall.

Gave meaning to my life,
Became as one,
This was the start,
Where at last it's begun.

One's Self

Relaxing beneath the autumn moon,
Humming along to some old tune,
Experiencing a feeling that once was lost,
Realizing it may not have been worth the cost.

To lose ones self and no longer feel,
Remembering that life once gave a thrill,
Yet somehow all seemed slowly to change,
Leaving one with a sense of not being the same,

Needing what later was found again,
Accepting that never again should life end,
Learning that love is the truest way to freedom,
Held within this autumn of the season.

A time of renewal at last has arrived,
Tears of joy are all I now cry,
Never knowing such wonder as I now do,
All came so fast and claimed my life anew,

Knowing I'm no longer a stranger who's lost,
That losing one's self is not worth the cost,
And realizing that in knowing and finding one's self,
Should in time be put above all else.

Enlightened

As I look out beyond,
Just over the horizon,
There's just a hint of light,
As the sun begins rising.

I know only one thing,
That this is home,
And a sense of such joy,
At not being alone.

I know this place,
It's where I belong,
The mountains surrounding,
The heart filled with song,

At last feeling love,
That once was forbidden,
And knowing within,
No longer is it hidden.

Calmness washes over me;
Heart and soul can be seen,
All it took was to follow,
The brightest sunbeam.

To search that horizon
And climb the high mountains,
Life is now overflowing,
Like the tears of a fountain.

A fulfillment unknown
Now seems so far in the past,
I've found who I am,
Am enlightened at last.

Love

Like the warmth of a fire,
Warming you deep to the core,
And a sense of excitement
With all it's allure,

Love takes control,
The temperatures rising,
You're floating above the clouds,
Before realizing.

At last you're alive,
Sensing so much more,
For now you feel love,
Completely to the core.

You no longer feel loneliness,
For now your heart is whole
With the one you wanted,
Who owns you heart and soul.

Renewal Of Heart

When the day at last comes,
And you've found where you belong,
Will it be all you expected it to be,
Will you soar and feel free?

The answers lie just before you;
Yet within sensing all that has yet to renew,
Many times have you wished and dreamed,
But your heart keeps faith and believes.

Will the one you love feel as you do,
Will this be a time for life to renew?
Who knows where your heart will lead you?
Just believe it will tell you true.

True love is there and can be found,
Even in simple words feel and sense all so profound.
The truth is always held within the heart and soul,
You must follow yourself to find the place to go.

Never again to not be allowed,
Finding that which is right and learning how.
For the love you have at last found to be true,
Is all that's needed for you to renew.

Rushing Toward The Unknowns

Life alone is a journey within itself,
Sitting high above upon a shelf.
It's given to each and everyone,
Can come or go with the rising sun.

Gathering energies held in the air,
When not all seems quite so fair.
Electricity seems lost within a warp,
Keeps one moving, wanting only to soar.

Just a look into the future,
Waiting only for the soul to nurture.
There will be found that which is close,
And what is needed the most.

I'll journey to the farthest reaches at last,
Listening within forgetting the past.
No longer alone in that universe beyond,
Now feeling the warmth of the sun.

To find you have reached that unknown,
Continuing to sense that what is just beyond.
Finding life within the boundaries of time,
Nothing co-exists, yet there seems to be rhyme.

Energies seep into soul and heart,
Now moving faster, coming closer to the start.
Soaring higher above the clouds,
Hearing only the music and no other sound.

The time has come to reach out and explore,
Even if afraid, I must dare to soar;
I've now found that which was there,
Life and the future have become more dear.

A Moment

A moment, a light, a path lies ahead,
Should I rest now or follow where led?
Cannot believe in that which is not there,
Yet have faith and becoming aware.

Caring not what may be
But following the heart where it leads,
There I will find happiness and love;
After all this is what I have wanted,

Searching not for what I don't deserve,
But willing to accept that which I have earned.
Listening carefully to the words as they are spoken,
With faith will have all that I was hoping.

A path left unused and covered over,
Is what you will find if it's discovered.
Follow the heart where it leads,
For there the words "I love you" will be seen.

Crossing Paths

Watching the sun and moon cross paths,
At that moment I knew our love would last.
Matters not what pain or hurt may arrive,
We'll trust one another as we stand side by side,

Filling the voids once felt within,
Knowing our hearts had the will to begin;
For never in life could there be another,
The universe pushed our paths together.

Accepting what is real and complete,
Sensing the heart of one another fulfilling our needs.
A bright glow from deep within,
Drew both souls together in the end.

They sensed the beginning of what was to come,
For in our hearts we knew we belonged,
Never looking back to what made the void begin,
And within the vastness of our hearts found it would never end.

As it was with the moon just a shadow over the sun,
We both sensed what there was yet to be discovered.
We are as shadows seeking out and crossing paths,
Within deep to the core have found a love that will eternally last.

Truths Of The Heart

There are many things,
Sensed yet hard to explain,
And too many dark clouds,
Seemingly the same.

Why do doubts flare up,
And come into play,
When there's so much in life,
That one wants only to stay?

Finding that where once you trusted,
And gave your heart completely,
Found it all within a moment,
But only to be deceived.

When you can't see realities
Within the darkness of these truths,
Is this why you grow weary and torn,
To find you are being abused?

Wanting only to feel,
Sensing the love now found,
Yet unsure just how,
To block out those dark clouds.

Dare not lose sight,
Of that which is felt within,
Yet knowing in your heart,
That all must depend.

Once was blinded with darkness,
That was held all around,
Dared not to breath,
Nor make a sound.

The day has at last come,
Can finally be seen and heard,
Thinking at last here it is,
Maybe just this once deserved.

Ideas and thoughts,
Of unknown origins appearing,
Within your heart and soul,
Still find fear within,

A fear that the love that is found,
Will one day be gone,
Unsure of these feelings,
Not wanting to be left alone.

A love so deeply felt,
Beckoning not wanting to lose sight,
For with true love,
Fear can be conquered within the light.

Will keep within the heart,
As never had before,
For now love no longer deceives,
Never again will close the door.

Shadows

Shadows cast,
From the past,
Pain comes,
Never belonged.

Anger flares,
The soul slowly dies,
No more tears,
Nothing left to cry.

Fire becomes hot,
And the heart breaks,
Listened to it once,
Knew it a mistake.

Dark clouds over,
Winds seem harsh,
Yet what is broken,
Lies within the heart.

Scars will heal,
Of this I am sure,
Yet must wonder
Just what occurred.

Reality takes control,
And tells the truth,
The shadows may win,
The heart may again lose.

Give that which is held,
Deeply within,
For if there be life,
Must find the end.

Love comes once,
No doubts at all,
Filling the heart and soul,
Will not again fall.

The Cage Of Time

The cage came open,
Now almost closed.
The world stands outside;
Within, your heart knows.

Sanctuary seemed lost,
Never to appear,
For now within
Are pain and fear.

Love came knocking
And was deeply felt,
Followed your heart,
Was true to your self.

Now is the time,
To shed such fears.
Scars will heal;
No more tears.

Love is true,
If held and shared,
Giving it your all,
Knowing you dare.

It will hold within
All that is wondrously good;
For when you said I do,
You knew you could.

The Quiet Haunting

Just a simple search for something,
Can lead you to a quiet haunting,
Never being sure of yourself,
Yet going far beyond above all else.

Cannot find what you seek,
Yet with faith that soon shall meet.
Looking across the far horizons,
A sense of self still is rising,

Taking you to unknown places,
Where life begins so many spaces.
No escaping who you are meant to be,
This in itself is what you must see.

Searching for what you have yet to get,
Just another so called mind set.
A break or crack held within you ,
Gave you the reason to look and move.

Yet a quiet haunting became a part,
Of what was always in your heart.
You had all along what you searched for,
So close that finally chapter and open the door.

The Sun

Beyond the reaches of the sun,
Within those outer boundaries of space,
That is where life once begun,
Finding a most wondrous place.

Use the stars to be your guide,
For there is radiance of colors to be seen;
Truth will be found, there's no place to hide,
Never a doubt, you have only to believe.

Yet within the spheres of the cosmos,
You can hear the music of time and space,
Finding only the realities wanted most,
For there's a release you'll find in no other place,

A vastness to explore, wanting only to be known,
Makes it a wondrous place to explore,
Singing out all of its cosmic song,
Now beyond boundaries again to soar.

One Love

There can be but one love,
Be it now or never,
Of this I am completely sure,
Just knowing it will be forever.

And yet here we are,
Caught up in such passion,
Wondering just when and where,
Unsure as to how it happened.

Really, there's to be no answer,
And so we may despair;
Yet here before us it all is,
So wonderful and yet so rare.

Accepting that nothing's to be the same
Within this love of ours,
Now that both have begun to change,
Happiness is once again ours.

Music of The Soul

Music fills the soul,
Felt deeply to the core.
Feet begin to waltz,
Taking over the floor,

Sailing with the rhythm,
Time having no bearing.
For you and only you
Are the one who's truly hearing.

Escape and release,
All is alive within.
No longer sensing sadness,
Nor finding an end.

A melody of love,
Filling the heart and soul.
This new sense of being,
Is one you want to know.

On the wings of life,
Sailing and feeling such peace,
A new way of being
Within finding release.

Music in the soul,
Singing its wondrous tune.
Now the floor is yours
Take hold and pursue.

The Window

When you look out
And the window seems dull,
That isn't the way
Life should be at all.

A sense of reality,
Needs to take place,
Giving you strength,
Of time and space.

To see what is there,
The beauty of love,
Gives you inner peace,
On the wings to sail above.

For within these realms
Of love and beyond,
Will endure what is,
And reach toward the sun.

For there light is held,
To be released if allowed,
Giving you warmth,
A sense of just how.

Now glance out the window,
Just once more and see,
Now all is becoming clear,
Showing you how life should be.

Magic Of Christmas

There's magic in the air
And snow on the ground;
Church bells are ringing,
What a beautiful sound.

Houses decorated,
With a wreath on the door,
Lights shining bright,
And presents galore.

Christmas music being sung,
And turkeys being roasted,
Homes filled with laughter
Of good health being toasted.

Children sneaking around,
To see what's being wrapped;
If you look quickly,
Will see them run in a snap.

Around the hearth,
Stories from the past being told,
So many wondrous tales,
Of Christmases long ago.

It's a magical time,
And love fills the air;
Memories unfold,
Some with a tear.

There's a familiar warmth,
That all hold dear;
It's Christmas time again,
All be of good cheer.

A Ghostly Night

When the moon is full,
And the air is quiet,
Listen to the wind,
Moving in flight.

Take heed what you hear,
And show no fear,
For the midnight hour,
Has now appeared.

Be watchful of eyes,
Peering in the night,
For they will see you
And give you a fright.

Stand very still,
And hold your ground;
Listen with care,
For the ghostly sounds.

It's the bewitching hour,
All is in darkness;
The soul and the heart,
Will soon feel the hardness.

As the moon peeks out,
Clouds move from the light;
Try not to scream,
For what is in sight.

All will be clear,
If you but wait;
Allow no warning,
This seals your fate.

So when the moon's full,
And the air is quiet,
Listen to the wind,
As it moves in flight.

Darkness

The blackest of black,
Came down from heaven,
With the fullness of darkness,
As rich as a raven.

The darkness of gloom,
Absorbing the light,
Wanting your soul,
Expecting no fight.

For today must find
What you're made of inside,
Sensing the way
Allowing the heart be your guide.

The heart runs cold,
The soul filled with fear;
There on your cheek,
Lies what's left of a tear.

Beyond you must reach,
To fight the darkness of hell;
You must accept what surrounds;
Otherwise, you will fail.

This darkest of dark
Will hinder your way;
You must soon find escape,
On this darkest day.

The moon in its fullness,
Casts a shadow of light;
The darkness can't bind you,
For it's now taken flight.

You are free to go
And can sense the path;
The light shines upon you,
No darkness can last.

Fall

Fall is upon us,
Bringing quiet wonder.
Colors so bright,
Now lie in each corner,

A kind of poetry
Held within the leaves,
Quietly blowing,
Whispering on the breeze.

A chill lies lightly,
Floating with the air,
Bringing in its wake,
A day clear and fair.

Colors so bright
Bring beauty to the trees,
And the seas seem to notice,
For now they flow free.

Clouds glide by
As the sun shines down,
And within the trees
Is a whispering sound.

For now fall has come,
And brought a new world,
Where snow will soon fall,
Coming down in a swirl.

Then fires will roar,
Giving us their warmth;
And friends will sit quietly,
Gathered around the hearth.

It's a time to rest,
And the world slows down,
For fall is upon us;
It quietly surrounds.

Window Of Time

Dedicated To The One Who Helped Me Climb Mountains: James Caprio

Within a window of time,
I can always find my way,
Finding many mountains to climb
And all within a day.

For time has a way of standing still,
Even when it's moving too fast;
Sometimes things seem unreal,
Yet most hide within our past.

Looking for the path that guides one,
High above what once was known.
Reaching for the warmth of the sun,
Knowledge must be found alone.

But within one's heart and soul
Is that which has always been there,
A newness deep within,
Moving forward without a tear.

Within a window of time,
I can always find my way.
Seek the highest mountain to climb,
And you'll find yourself in a day.

Alive

The world is alive;
Can you not hear
The birds as they sing,
Wings spread without fear?

The wind as it blows,
Whistles through the trees,
Telling its tales
Of life as it should be.

The sun shining bright
Brings with it life,
Rains fall from heaven
In a circle of light.

Night will soon come;
With it comes such splendor:
Moon and stars above,
Skies dark as a cinder.

Life holds its truths;
Heart and soul are as one,
And here you will dwell,
Knowing life has begun.

The world is alive,
Held within your grasp;
Shed no more tears,
The time has come to pass.

Kindred Spirit

A kindred spirit
Flies on the wind,
A soul in flight,
Ready to descend,

Finding the path,
Sensed so right,
A yearning within
To find the light.

No longer bound,
Nor left alone,
It feels such life,
On the breeze a song.

A whisper heard,
Deep in the heart,
I have seen the way,
Found a new start.

A kindred spirit,
Free to sail,
At last sense the wonder,
Light showing the trail.

The Inner Self

Within that inner web we weave,
We wonder at times what others might see.
Will it be the good we hold so dear,
Or the pain we dare not share.

Many times we try to hide
Exactly what we feel inside.
Yet in that one moment of despair,
The feelings we have seem to appear.

What's felt within our hearts and souls,
May leave us very much exposed.
Just how we choose to handle it,
Can fill us with so much regret.

But if the one who sees us exposed
Understands he won't go.
Beside you he will take a stand,
And never leave you for he's a true friend.

Remembered Time

I remember a time,
As a little girl growing up,
Couldn't wait till the day,
I'd be a grown-up.

Those days are long gone
And so is that goal,
To return to those days,
Would be worth more than gold.

Days filled with the sun,
A time for fun and play,
It's rather funny now,
Looking back to those days.

Experience has its virtues,
And we all must live and learn;
When I was a little girl,
Playing was my only concern.

Now those days are gone,
Have only the memories to keep,
Would not change a thing,
In my heart will always be.

At last the time came
When I was a grown-up,
And felt love and contentment
Found in all of us.

Memories of past and present,
Will continue to be there;
For with our own children
We give part of us and share.

The Poet

Some call me poet,
I know not why,
I write the words,
At times I cry,

Writing what I feel
So deeply within,
And with these words
Find closure and end.

Still they come,
These words I write,
Sometimes show too much
What I sense in the light.

But the words come swiftly,
This I still can't understand,
I share my whole heart,
I take another's hand.

The words show truths,
Or at least what I see;
In them I give,
A part of me.

I am who I am,
Can be nothing more,
It began in my heart,
When love opened the door.

I try sometimes to hide,
And not share too much,
Yet within my words
Find another's heart to touch.

A poet I may be,
Then again maybe not;
But what I share,
I've given it all I've got.

Aunt Doris

(Dedicated to a wonderful lady who passed away in her 88th year)

As the wind whispers
And the hour draws near,
I need my rest,
No longer in fear.

The light has shown,
My path is lit;
I spread my wings,
My time well spent.

I gave my love
To all who knew me
And in return
Received love I could see.

So dry your eyes,
Shed no more tears,
For I am free,
Sensing no fear.

Memories are clear
And all is bright;
I'm flying now,
Moving toward the light.

Remember me in good times,
And accept all that was bad
But within your heart,
Never feel sad.

For now I see
And can hear so clear,
I'm spreading my wings
Without any fear.

I'm with you always,
Watching those I love;
Now I'm happy,
Sailing with the doves.

Ice

In the heat of the summer,
Sensing warmth all around,
Standing and listening,
You hear not a sound;

Wishing for the coolness,
That's a long way off,
Holding back it's frosty ice,
Snowy fields, white and soft.

Taking in the boundaries
Surrounding your soul
And sensing calmness,
The coolness makes you whole.

Sweat glistening across your brow,
And pours down your back,
Wanting only to end the suffering,
Burning like coal, dark and black.

At last there's a frost,
Pure and clear on the ground,
A coolness in the air,
A chill all around.

No longer a fire, burning within;
The time has come with ease,
A shimmer of content,
Cool as a winter's breeze.

Christmas Wonders

Look out your window,
And see the lights,
Glistening on snow,
So pure and white.

Decorations are hung,
For all to see,
A winter wonderland,
Lots of Christmas trees.

People singing out,
With joy in their hearts,
All began long ago,
A star was the start.

Children laughing and playing,
Being good as they can
Because it's Christmas time,
Santa's coming again.

Presents are wrapped,
With bows and pretty ribbon;
Hearts open up,
It's love they are giving.

So look out your window,
And see the lights,
Glistening on snow,
So pure and white.

The Mirror

There's a mirror on the right wall,
I look at my image completely in awe.
Wondering what that really reflects,
Can I truly find my dreams? Most unsure yet.

Who is this person staring back at me?
Why can't I look and honestly see?
Am I a good person or am I bad,
These questions make me feel sad.

Not understanding who I am in my heart,
And yet I know it's time to start.
Must gather my inner strength and fight,
Knowing by this, I will do what is right.

Never again to be held in a cage with bars,
Now I know I can fly so very far.
Alert to all the dangers of the turmoil inside,
Yet knowing now cannot ever truly hide.

A woman stares back with tears in her eyes,
What is it that makes her so sad? Why does she cry?
An urgency I sense within this person in the mirror,
Yet I see a woman left unprepared.

A new light seems to shine just behind,
She can not feel it, is she so very blind?
Yet not quite understanding what is wanted of her,
Gives way to fear and all that makes her insecure.

But also can see the heart and the soul,
This is where she will find true love and her goal.
Now reality seems to take hold,
I am that person now in control.

Dreams Of Hope

Within dreams there lies hope;
Listening to a hum only you can hear,
You find ideas with which you might cope,
Knowing that something wonderful is near.

Feeling such love within its presence,
Now finding it's completely enveloping the mind,
Yet dare I go after that which is sensed,
Even if unsure it's the right time.

Move forward in this world of dreams,
Believing you are someone,
Daring never to feel that need to leave,
Accepting you can move beyond,

Feeling a need, yet wanting to hide,
Sensing at last there are no more tears,
Wanting to the keep the dreams and never to cry,
Accepting what is without fear left inside.

The Wedding

As I watch and listen,
I hear the angels sing.
Within the circle, I glimpse
An exchange of two rings.
Is this love or so much more,
Will it last forever?
These things we do not know;
Only time will show.
I feel tears of joy,
Fresh as the morning dew.
They sought out each other,
Now they say "I do".
Two hearts twined as one
Beat together new as dawn.
Never to be alone;
Two souls become as one.

Time

Time grows short,
I know not why;
Look to the stars,
Look to the sky.

The answers are there,
Of this I am sure,
A moment, a minute,
Feeling secure.

No place to run,
I will not hide;
The moon is full,
No tears to cry.

I'll find the way,
When the sun does rise,
I'll follow the path,
Keeping life inside.

Time will fade,
But not this day,
A path to travel,
Have found the way.

When The Lights Go Out

When the lights go out,
And you're alone in the dark,
Don't be afraid,
Look in your heart.

Feel the energy within,
Let it explode,
Then, my friend,
You'll know where to go.

Life isn't always a reality
You might want to face,
But it is within this truth
Will sense the light fine as lace.

Touch that which you see,
Feel that which you don't,
Then you will see it all,
You're not meant to be alone.

Take it all in and live,
And then you my friend,
Will at last move forward,
Finding it all in the end.

Time grows so very short,
But only if you allow it,
So don't stand in the dark;
Fly and sail with the clouds.

I Am Thankful

I am thankful for the rainbows of life
And all things simple and nice,
The wonder of babies being born
And even my coat, old and worn.

I am thankful for a child's smile,
And being able to walk the long mile
Where snow glistening on the ground
Still continues to keep me spellbound.

I am thankful for the love I feel
When I am well and even if ill,
Where singing out, even off key,
I can still smile and continue to sing.

I am thankful for being able to laugh,
As time closes in and the past is the past,
Laughing and feeling joy within,
There is always a reason to rejoice, again and again.

I am thankful for friends by my side,
Always there with hello, never a goodbye;
For life is worthy of enjoying and living,
And warmth fills the heart for sharing and giving.

Spreading Wings in Flight

In as many days and as many nights,
I've learned to spread my wings in flight
Beyond the realms I knew not of;
I can float on the wind and sail like a dove.

At last becoming aware of what there is to be,
I move further out, yet closer, that I might see.
There on the horizon is a beacon of light;
There I will become whole in flight.

No one to stop this course I have chosen;
For now my heart's open, no longer closing.
The path, no matter how far or how long;
This is my way, this is where I belong.

Never before allowed just to be,
Here I am flying across the sea,
The wind at my back helping me fly,
No longer feeling my heart die.

Coming alive, feeling life within,
Gives cause to move, awakened on the wind;
For there on the horizon is that glimmer of light,
I'll find my way as I spread wings in flight.

Candle Of Light

One year following the Sept. 11 tragedy

We have lit our candles and said our prayers,
Now we've all become more aware,
Innocence seems to have been taken away,
Yet in this world we all must stay.

What began in the past is now our future;
Hopefully in this we will finally begin to nurture,
Clinging and holding to those we love
And saying prayers to our God above.

Let there be peace in this world we pray,
And allow those in pain to find their way.
Never again to look on such horrors,
Let us now look to the many tomorrows.

There's an underlining truth to what has been seen,
Let the tears of heaven begin to clean.
An acceptance is needed so we can move on,
Forget hatred, and look to the sun.

Healing within needs to start in our hearts,
In this we'll find a wondrous new start
And acceptance that as people we're free,
It's time to allow the past to just be.

Magical Stars

The magic of life is held in the stars,
Look to the heavens they really aren't far;
Cast all worries and doubts aside;
Just look above, and at last you will fly.

Feel the rhythm of all the universe,
You'll feel the pull with such force,
You'll soar to the highest reaches of the sky,
This you must trust and give it a try.

If you really want what life has to give,
You must first begin to live.
Fill your soul with love of self;
This must be done above all else.

It's a wondrous feeling you will feel within,
But first accept and then you may begin.
Time is filled with the magic you need;
In this you will finally succeed.

So look to the stars and know they are there,
You soon will become more than just aware.
Sense all the magic held in a star,
This is truly who you are.

Hello Star

Hello Star, is this to be the night,
When I may take my first flight,
Finally allowed to spread my wings,
Able at last to fly and sing.

Am I to come and visit with you,
And will I see all my wishes so new?
May I sit upon your farthest point,
Or is your light merely a taunt?

Let me know if you heard my wishes,
Or did they pass you by?
Quietly each night I seek you out,
And never do I cry.

So hello again, my brightest star.
Is this truly to be my night?
I'm at last ready to unfold my wings,
And begin my journey held in light.

By Chance

I walked alone,
The road was steep,
And then by chance,
We did meet.

Finding one another,
Soul for soul,
Never again,
To walk alone.

Two ships sailing,
Passing at night,
We came together,
Held in moonlight.

You held my heart,
As I held yours,
You gave me it all,
As we soared.

The Song Beyond

As I wondered in a time unknown,
The sounds were able to touch my heart;
I listened carefully to the new song,
Allowing it to draw closer that we might never part,

Feeling it within the core of my soul,
Allowing it to take me to far reaches, I went,
Knowing that it's at last time to go,
Accepting this was the place I was sent.

Tears streamed a line upon my face,
As I sensed reality I'd never known,
Knowing my heart belonged to this place,
Sensing safe haven in this far beyond.

Carefully finding my true bearings,
Feeling sounds within my heart and soul,
Realizing what it was that I was hearing,
Taking me and making me whole.

At last I could feel the beauty within,
My heart and soul finding harmony as one,
Feeling such inner peace again,
Singing and moving into the far beyond.

Time Of Reflection

There's a time in life when one must rest,
Disregarding all that seems unjust,
A spiritual time in which we know,
And we go about it oh so slow;

A time to sit back and listen,
Remembering, not knowing what we're missing.
A time to reflect on days gone by,
Yet wondering how the time did fly;

A time to remember one's beginnings,
Yet never knowing when they're ending;
To follow those dreams we once thought lost,
Caring not about the cost;

Casting aside doubts we once had,
Knowing ourselves and not feeling bad;
Reconsidering what we once wanted,
Never feeling sad or haunted.

A simple reflection is all that's needed,
Like planting a garden and getting it seeded.
Yes, it's time for mind and body to rest,
Have had a wonderful life and all the best.

The Grandfather Clock

The grandfather clock began to strike twelve,
I knew in my heart no more time to dwell.
A quiet sense of calm I felt within,
Is it my time to live again?

I'll leave my bonds of time behind,
Seeing ahead and not moving forward blind.
There's a brook in the meadow that begins to flow,
Gently and quietly moving forward slow,

A grove of trees over the hill beyond;
That's where first love so brightly dawned.
Within the center of the old shade trees,
That's where my heart was at last set free.

Allowed to sit with him I love and feel,
Knowing this sense of being is real,
No longer alone waiting for the moment to come,
I've found true love and the place I belong.

As the grandfather clock again strikes twelve,
I've nothing to fear: here is where I must dwell.
A sense of belonging heart and soul combined
In love that will take me to the end of time.

Moving Forward

As we look to the past,
Yet reach out for the tomorrows,
We sense our beginnings,
Even if met with sorrows.

We sense that which was,
And feel what is now,
And yet within our hearts,
Move forward somehow.

Our souls are filled with life,
From which we draw strength,
And gather our loved ones,
Keeping them at arms length.

Love close by our side,
Through smiles and tears,
Never allowing life to go,
Nor letting in any fears.

There is so much to be said,
Must find the time,
The many tomorrows will come,
Hurrying quickly by.

Tomorrow

What would happen tomorrow,
If I weren't there?
Would you be worried,
Would you be scared?

If I left no forwarding address,
What would you say?
Would you put it off,
Till the next day?

Suppose I leave no note,
For you to find;
Would you forget me,
And leave me behind?

If I came back to you,
Would we start anew?
All of these questions,
I am asking of you.

So if by chance,
I'm not there,
Remember my love,
Not all is clear.

Do You Believe

Do You Believe
Do you believe,
In the things you see,
Even if unsure,
In that which must be?

Do you believe,
In what you can't conceive?
Even in darkness,
Light will help you see.

Do you believe,
In a universe far beyond,
Where the sun rises,
And all life has begun?

Do you believe,
In love at first sight,
When within your heart,
All feels so right?

Do you believe,
That where there is a past,
There's a future,
As yet to be had?

Do you believe,
Beauty is held in all things,
Even if not as it seems,
Nor ever the same?

Do you believe,
In yourself above all else,
Like a rose pedal,
A bud within itself?

Do you believe,
These are the questions of life?
We must ask them,
Even if not perfect nor even precise.

Searching

Through the windows of my soul,
I know for sure I am whole,
No bars or locks can keep me in,
For at last my heart can mend.

There are many things to be learned,
I'll not turn my back nor ever return.
The things I know best can be expanded,
And within my world a new beginning.

What ever happens and what will be,
All I can do is run toward it and see.
I want to feel with all my soul,
The things in life, all there to behold.

Can it be so wrong to want these things,
To at last see and never to be the same?
I'm searching from within to find my way,
It may not happen, at least not this day.

But if I look within and try very hard,
I know that one day I will find my star.
Even if not perfect, that's ok,
At least I tried without delay.

Emotions and feelings are ready to go,
And if I don't do something, will soon explode.
So as I look in my heart for my own way,
I feel sure it will come even if not this day.

Awake My Love

Awake my love, it's time to rise,
Don't let life just pass you by.
There's much to be seen this day,
All life's joys with which to play.

Take my hand and walk with me,
There are many things you must see.
Sense the love and what is to be,
This at last will set you free.

Feel the breeze upon your face,
This is the time and the right place.
Feel the warmth enveloping you,
Take it all in , it's all so new.

It has been there all along for you and me,
Just reach out and feel and try to see.
Is this not what you've been looking for,
I believe life can be so much more.

Whisper to me your wishes my dear,
Will always listen and try to hear.
Here for you as I always am,
A bird in flight without any sound.

What I see in life wish only to share,
All that is love and so very near.
My heart and soul are yours to keep,
So rest now my love, it's time to sleep.

Beauty of the Butterfly

As a butterfly lands near the pond,
I can't help but gently respond.
It holds such beauty and such grace,
Seems its tiny wings are made of lace.

As I watch it flutter here and there,
I become alive and more aware.
Its beauty it seems is all it needs,
Yet this cannot be all there is to see.

The breeze softly caresses its wings,
And it closes over the butterfly, so it seems.
Can almost feel the freedom as in flight,
And can float along within that light.

Butterfly kisses can be astounding,
When first you feel and your heart begins pounding,
But there it is in all its glory and grace,
Must be worthy of the light and place.

One Moment

The moment is gone,
No longer to be seen,
It came and it went,
As if a light beam.

Flew high above,
Here, there and yonder,
No longer in awe,
Left only with wonder.

To measure one's way,
And find what is there,
You must look above,
Become more aware.

The time that's left,
Leaves one dismayed,
You wish on a star,
You wait for the day.

The moment is gone,
Yet will be seen again,
Just reach for the stars,
Hold out your hand.

My World

Is this my world,
Can it truly be mine?
I feel such loneliness,
A sense of lost time.

Not yet prepared,
Trying to understand,
My love was given,
Sinking as if quick sand.

But here I am,
Thinking of all that's around,
Searching the clouds,
As they sink and surround.

Can it not be,
Just once and forever,
A life complete,
Becoming much clearer.

Awaiting just once to be,
Could it not be held,
In my heart such wonder,
Might I again fail?

Will not again allow,
Seeking the sun,
To shed light complete,
Opening up the clouds.

For I won't give up,
Memories are now,
No longer looking back,
Will fly above the clouds.

Truth of the Heart

Can there be love,
Without compromise,
Looking in the heart,
Trying to be honest?

This question is asked,
But there are no answers,
Can real love,
Allow one to surrender?

So simple I have found love,
That I truly don't know,
Yet within my heart,
Does anyone really know?

Would it not be simpler,
If you could read another?
A sense of awe held within,
Coming from the another.

There are no answers,
No matter how hard you look,
People close themselves off,
As if closing a book.

But when you find love,
A sense of peace above all others,
Comes to you within,
Sharing yourself with another.

So seek out the answers,
Looking deeply within,
And remember love comes but once,
This is your answer in the end.

Charlotte Ann Caprio resides in Arizona with her husband, Jim. She was born and raised in South Carolina, living there until she met her husband almost three years ago. Most of her grandchildren and children live in S.C. and she visits the State as often as she can. This is her first book. It started out with one thought in mind, and that was to leave a legacy to her grandchildren. As she grew, the book grew, and it became apparent that it was much more than a legacy. It became a way that she would give her grandchildren some insight as to who she is. Being Southern born, she knows the importance of tradition and family.